C000112122

Leading Worship

Ten Simple Truths

Marc Millan

References:

1. Bob Sorge- Author, speaker, www.bobsorge.com

2. A.W. Tozer- Preacher, Author, www.awtozer.org

3. Larry Osborne- Author, Pastor, speaker, www.larryosbornlive.com

4. Simon Sinek- Author, speaker, www.startwithwhy.com

5. Dr. Henry Cloud- Clinical psychologist, theologian, author, speaker. www.drcloud.com

6. Craig Groeschel- Pastor, Author, www.craiggroeschel.com

Copyright 2019 © Marc Millan | ISBN: 9781074717483

All rights reserved. No part of this publication may be reproduced, distributed, or transmitted in any form or by any means, including photocopying, recording, or other electronic or mechanical methods, without prior written permission of the publisher, except in the case of brief quotations embodied in critical reviews and certain other non commercial uses permitted by copyright law.

For more information About.me/marcmillan, Instagram@marcmillan

Unless otherwise indicated, scripture quotations were taken from the New International Version of the Bible, the New Living Translation of the Bible, the New American Standard Bible, New English Translation, English Standard Version, The God's Word Translation- all copyright © 1973,1978, 1984, 2011 by Biblica, Inc

Table of Contents:

This book is dedicated to every Worship Leader.

You are loved, you are so much more than your gifts. You are a mighty child of God. Rise up a warrior. Strong in mind, tender in heart. I believe in you. God designed you to reflect His glory so allow His glory to be seen through you. Walk in faith, not in fear. Allow God's love to transform you. Embrace the process. Enjoy the journey and above all, be great at what you do because you are amazing.

INTRODUCTION

My journey as a worship leader started in a season where I was just trying to survive the music business. I was signed to Sony-BMG Latin at the time and I was writing songs, recording demos, traveling back and forth to A&R meetings and I found myself in a hard place. You see my whole life had led me to this point. I always wanted to use my gifts in music to impact people. Something about singing and playing instruments gave me purpose and life.

After I signed the record deal, that purpose became confusing and clouded as I was striving to write hit songs, to brand myself, to prove myself as an artist. All of a sudden what was once a pure passion and gift had become… corrupted.

Soon after, the record business became very shaky. Napster was being sued by the major music labels for something called "peer to peer" file sharing a.k.a downloading music. My future in the record biz seemed on the shelf. The five major Latin music labels got nervous and began laying people off and within months, it looked like my record, which was complete at the time, would never come out. This led me to a very broken and disappointed place.

It was in this broken season that God called me into service at a local church. I started out just wanting to be a part of a worship team as a back up singer and musician but God had other plans. Within months I was leading teams and leading services.

I didn't know what being a worship leader meant at all. I knew music, I knew arranging, I knew the language of making great music and I had a professional background but worship? Worship was a mystery to me, never mind leading it.

As time went on I began to learn more about worship music and I also began to grow in my personal worship. My understanding of God's word grew and God began putting a passion for worship leading in my heart.

This book is a reflection of those lessons, those truths that transformed me from a person singing songs of worship to becoming a worshiper. This book is written as a practical field guide. I kept the contents focused and straightforward. I also added three questions at the end of each chapter. I believe these discussion questions can help unpack each truth as you read and process them. As I began to serve as a worship leader I learned a lot about what it is and what it means to lead worship services and serve with teams that do it.

I hope to pass along a series of simple truths designed for worship leaders. With the increase of worship music becoming more vivid in the church globally, what I see as a worship reformation in the church, the worship leader role has become a central part of the local church over the last few decades.

I hope you can greatly benefit from what I've been able to learn. You are a spiritual leader, a musical shepherd, pastoring people that you serve with and the congregation God has entrusted to you. I have learned the truths listed here through many different experiences, personal devotion, personal pain, Biblical study, failures and successes, reading lots of books, reflection and prayer, and from being mentored from some of the brightest leaders in ministry.

These topics are personal to me and these themes are founded and rooted in God's Word, which is the final authority on all matters of worship. Although I have narrowed it down to just ten, please know that there are many more truths to discover and apply in your own journey and calling. Like anything, there are also many pitfalls we discover as well. Thankfully God is merciful and patient with us.

I also hope this little hand guide can be a refresher for both those who've been devoted to this area of ministry for some time and also a helpful guide for those who are just now stepping into the calling of leading worship. I don't consider the call to be a worship leader a simple task; I do believe it to be one of the hardest of ministry callings. Worship leaders stand between Jesus and the bride of Christ week after week, either pointing people towards Jesus or towards something else.

As Bob Sorge says, "it's not business, it's personal"[1]. Worship is personal to God, it's weaved throughout all of scripture starting from Genesis with Adam and Eve, through Abraham's journey up a mountain. When Abraham worshiped there was no typical worship set up, no music playing, no lights, no songs and no sermon. There was just Abraham's heart settled in God's character and promise, offering his own son as a sacrifice and the conviction to respond to who God is in worship.

We see in scripture how music stepped into the picture much later on with instruments, songs, poems, musicians, singers, leaders, and choirs, all organized for a purpose. Just as we read in the book of Revelation, chapter five where all living creatures, all the elders, saints and angels gather in wonder and awe to worship The Lamb that was slain, who was and is and is to come, our King Jesus.

—

Selah.

So, is leading worship a big deal? It is to God and therefore, my hope is that this little book can become a tool for you throughout your seasons of leading, your seasons of receiving revelation and through the seasons of dryness and doubt. May the grace and mercy of God keep you faithful to His heart, the One who has called you, so that you can serve faithfully and minister to Him and bless the people in His name. I'll be praying for you and cheering you on until the day that we are all gathered around the throne to worship the wonderful and precious name of Jesus together in eternity.

CHAPTER 1

WORSHIP IS UNTO THE LORD

Where should the energy and focus of our worship get directed?

Deuteronomy 10:8 At that time the LORD set apart the tribe of Levi to carry the ark of the covenant of the LORD to stand before the LORD to minister to Him and to bless the people in his name, to this day. (**ESV**)

What is worship? Is it the first part of a service at a church? Is it found in a private space with the lights off or dim? Is it a lifestyle? Just what is worship anyway? Let's start to unpack this by taking a look at its first appearance found In **Genesis 22**. In this chapter we discover the main character, Abraham is about to respond to God in worship in what I would consider a very difficult situation. He has been asked by God to sacrifice his beloved son, Isaac. In this chapter we find a strong and clear picture of not only what true worship is but the Gospel as well.

Abraham had a personal encounter with God by this point in the Bible and after years of enjoying the promise of God, God wanted to test His heart again (because no one really knows their own heart). We all know the story from that point - Abraham decisively packs up all his stuff and heads out, taking his son Isaac with him. He grabs the dead wood, the knife and all that would be needed for this sacrifice, which doesn't look like a normal Sunday worship service in our culture.

You see what is really important to catch here is that Abraham committed to worship God because He knew who God was, not just what He did. Worship is personal to God and it was personal to Abraham too, this time requiring the sacrifice of his own son. He wasn't carrying his backpack for other people, nor was he trying to make the people around him comfortable when responding with this sacrifice. In fact his entire focus wasn't on people at all, it was on the Lord God Almighty. Abraham was focused on worshiping God. He followed through with his sacrifice with a surrendered love for God, which is the essence of real worship. Abraham's heart responded to who he knew God to be.

Worship is when our heart and life are fully engaged and surrendered to God. However, not out of obligation; worship is not a forced action, pressured or manipulated. It's a response that springs up from the heart, out of love and adoration.

I define worship this way: **Worship is a response to the magnificence of God as revealed in Christ Jesus**. Worship should include some form of expression like the use of hands, singing, music and movement but it MUST include the inner person's willing surrender to God in love. Our spirit must be engaged for it to be true worship. If the heart is not engaged, it's simply not worship because worship is a heart response unto the Lord.

Worship is about delighting in God, the very joy of knowing who He is and us responding to that with our very hearts and lives. Worship is unto God, *for people*, not to people. Revelation and response; I'm afraid many times we confuse song services with worship. A person can participate in singing, clapping and even moving to songs and music and never enter into true worship. What would be the point of singing the songs if the heart isn't living the songs? Our lives always sound louder than the words we sing and the lives we live become our life song. True worship is a matter of the heart because all of life's direction springs up from the heart of the person. Whatever has the heart is the center of worship.

True worship is when the whole person is willingly responding in love and delight to the revelation of who God is; when we are seeing and enjoying His attributes, His magnificence, His wonder and especially the revelation of God through Christ Jesus. Worship isn't the appetizer in the service setting up the meal. If the sermon is the meal, then worship is enjoying the fellowship of the person you are eating with. Abraham wasn't setting up the offering for the person after him or going through the motions, he was engaged because it was insanely personal. Does worship music help people receive the Word? I believe it can when God touches it because when we truly worship our hearts are re-centered around our purpose IN Him. In worship we get realigned with God's heart. It humbles our hearts and centers us to properly and readily receive His Word for us. Ultimately, true worship always leads to mission because when we encounter God's heart we regain our purpose in Him.

Too often I discover that many singers and musicians join teams of praise and worship with a genuine desire to serve the Lord, however their focus and energy becomes misplaced on what people think and how people will react to their "performance." Let's be clear... worship is unto the Lord. We minister to God and He ministers to us. We ascribe worth to Him and He reveals our worth in Christ. We pour out our love on Him and He pours out His love on us. We bless Him and He blesses us- this is the joy of worship. We regain our purpose and perspective when we worship. This is how God designed it to be from the very beginning.

Worship is unto God; it's never to the people. However, when it is focused on the people there is actually another word used in that instance- it's called idolatry. Worship is to God, for people. We direct our worship to God. We offer ourselves in worship and surrender our worship to God. Worship benefits the worshiper.

The word ministry means service, but our heart's worship is never to be directed at people. It's directed and intended, reserved and prepared for God alone, this is of the utmost importance. One thing I need to point out here is that our talents and gifts are not offerings. WE are the offering. Christ has fully satisfied our debt and all we can bring to God is ourselves as the offering. We are living sacrifices before God and to live for him is the offering. God doesn't need our worship. On the contrary, we engage in worship so that we can be reminded about how great and awesome He is.

In order to ensure this process remains pure we must set all of our focus on Jesus. All of scripture was written to point us to our need for Jesus and reveal Jesus. Therefore, our worship must be founded and focused on glorifying Jesus. It's important that we don't portray God in vague terms, abstract feelings and metaphors of earthly love. I believe there is room for creative expressions of God in the body of Christ, but if we are discussing true worship- Jesus must be at the center of it all. Why might you ask? God's Word makes it clear in **Colossians 1:15** that Jesus is the image of the invisible God. He is the perfect revelation of who God is to us. Jesus came to make clear all that was confusing about God. As A.W. Tozer says, "Jesus came to convert rebels into worshipers."[2] Jesus said, "No one comes to the Father but through Me." He is the author and finisher of our faith. He is before all things and all things were created in Him, by Him and for Him that He may be all in all. True worship is about Jesus.

Christ has made this possible. Christ is the focus and is the reason for the service, the song, the music, the singing, and He is the why of worship! God has set it up so that we can minister to Him directly.

Don't miss the importance and privilege of this point. God could have saved us in His mercy and never allowed us to come near to Him or even minister to Him. He has granted us bold access through Jesus.

This is where the Old Testament priests got it wrong (except for a select few). They put their focus on the work of ministry and the activity of worship and lost the purpose and privilege of it. In other words, they were working in ministry without enjoying the wonder of being able to minister to God directly. They were working in the temple, but not serving the Lord. I fear sometimes we put so much focus and time in the preparation of the music and ignore the preparation of the heart.

God is seeking true worshipers. More importantly, He has given us access to His presence, and we can worship Him directly and enjoy all of who He is at any time. What a tragedy to have the incredible privilege to minister before the throne of God and yet end up pouring all of our energy towards people. No, beloved, we are worshipers of God. We minister to an audience of One; the only hands cheering us on that matter are nail scarred hands. So, how do people benefit in our times of worship? I am glad you asked. It is out of the overflow of our ministry unto God that we are able to bless people.

Our sincere worship of God invites, inspires and teaches others how to engage in worshiping God. We are "Royal Priests" for God. The word Priest is rooted in the idea of "bridge builders." In Christ we have been born again to rule and reign, worship and serve as Kings and Priests. We minister to God and we help people. Worship is never to be forced on people; it's not to be demanding or used to manipulate people's response. Worship is a voluntary act.

Through the demonstration of our own personal worship, we lead, inspire, invite and encourage people to engage with God, but they have to choose to worship on their own. The people of God benefit from our own personal praise as we minister to God. God always responds to the needs of His people. Therefore, we minister to God in faith, believing for God to move in and through our worship, releasing our praise over the atmosphere so others can join in and receive from God what only God can provide.

In corporate worship gatherings, as we minister to God, we help God's church regain their understanding of their purpose through teaching and showing what it looks like. We help them remember that in Christ they too are called to be ministers, called to be a chosen people unto God, Royal Priests set apart for His glory and purpose.

Ultimately, by ministering to God first, we get His heart for people. As we draw closer to Him and He imparts His heart into us, we gain the clarity for what daily ministry should look like. We carry His presence everywhere we go, we release the Kingdom of God everywhere we go and as we are transformed by His love and heart we bless people in His name.

Study questions: WORSHIP IS UNTO THE LORD

Just how important to you is the response of the people when you are leading worship?

Is your personal worship time focused on learning worship music or focused on knowing who God is?

After leading worship, who is the person you aim to please the most?

CHAPTER 2

CONNECTED TO THE VINE

Where do we find our strength and vitality in leading worship?

John 15:5 I am the vine; you are the branches. Whoever abides in me and I in him, he it is that bears much fruit, for apart from me you can do nothing. (**ESV**)

In Florida we have many storms over the summer. Some of those storms are winds that come in and push our trees violently back and forth bending them and many times snapping off branches and palm leaves. Have you ever seen a branch lying on the ground in a park after a storm has passed? If it's been sitting several days in the dry heat it doesn't have much color. Unless it has just broken off, the color starts to fade to a pale brown, the leaves become flaky and brittle and if you pick it up, you will realize they are very easy to snap. A dead branch is lifeless. There aren't many uses for dead branches.

When we are disconnected from the True Vine, we are like dead branches, trying to produce life without having life flowing in us and through us. Leading others in worship requires spiritual vitality. Spiritual vitality flows like a river and we are the vessels of God's power and grace. His strength flows in and through our lives, our words, our songs, our music and our actions and if there is going to be a reflection of Kingdom vitality in what we do, we must be connected to the True Vine, Jesus.

People so often confuse activity with productivity. Sometimes they do look the same, however, over time you can see the difference. Both require our attention, energy and focus but only one of them produces fruit. Jesus spoke often of fruit, a good tree cannot produce bad fruit and a bad tree cannot produce good fruit. The question we must be willing to ask and answer is; are we producing good fruit?

God is much more interested in who we are becoming than what we are accomplishing. What we do for God can never exceed or be separated from who we are called to be in Him. In the end it's who we are that matters over what we do. Let me say it this way... your worth and value as a person is not defined by your talent. Your worth and value as a person are not defined by what you do. Your gifts and talents are not your identity, at least I hope. Wherever you feel self worth or value from is where you get your identity. What you do is your function. My gifts and talents don't define my identity; my identity is rooted in the person of Jesus Christ, I am in Him, He is in me.

The Scriptures declare that I am a Royal Priest; a minister unto God and this defines my relational standing with God. My function does not define my standing with God. What I do in the kingdom is attached to my purpose (how and where my gifts and talents function).

The reason I want to unpack this a little bit is because this is where it can all go wrong for those of us focused on ministry, especially anyone who serves on a team that leads others in worship. We can become so busy with preparing, rehearsing, learning, practicing and executing all the details musically. However, how much time have we decided to spend in prayer, in personal worship, in getting our hearts prepared to serve and minister to the Lord? We forget that worship is a spiritual experience, not a musical one. Beware of becoming an accidental Pharisee, where your public worship is more active and refined than your private worship. If we aren't careful, we can get really good at engaging in worship only when we serve the masses and disregard the personal pursuit of Jesus when we aren't using our gifts on the platform.

Jesus is the purpose and focus of our worship. Jesus is the True Vine and in Him we find all that we need for life and godliness. He sustains us to do what He called us to do, but more importantly, He sustains us to be what He has redeemed us to be. Just like a branch has to stay connected to the tree to flourish, we have to stay connected to the vine in order to flourish as sons and daughters of the Most High. Who we are matters more than what we do. Trust me; character over accomplishments is what matters to God. When we are in glory and stand before the throne, who you are will matter much more than what you accomplished.

I know that sounds hard to hear and accept but so many people in ministry lose sight of the fact that we are saved to belong to Jesus, not to become workers for Jesus. God isn't facing an unemployment crisis, madly recruiting a bunch of workers. It's out of our daily and personal worship and our daily devotion to Christ that we grow in His image and heart, and out of that, we are aligned to His purpose. Again, when we worship God we regain our purpose and perspective in Him. It's out of this relationship that we enter into good works, saved for good works, not *by* good works, what I have done will be evaluated and rewarded, yes but my resume won't count for much when I stand before God's throne. However, it is who I am in Christ that matters on that day. If Christ is in me, whatever I do should reflect His image, His heart and bear His good fruit and good fruit comes from good roots.

When I am continually rooted in the Vine, His nature, His glory and His heart will be shown in all I do. When it comes to leading worship, we are pouring something out of us. We are engaging and releasing and we can become depleted really quickly. Since we are the offering in our worship, we can ignore the health of the vessel in the process.

Serving and giving of our time must flow out of our connection to Jesus; this is the most important thing for our soul and ministry. I've heard of too many leaders who had incredible gifts, talents and amazing platforms of influence that ignored their own personal connection to Jesus to chase ministry. The results are always sad; the fruit of their lives was stained with pride, sin, anger, arrogance, chaos, destruction, relationships ruined and years of tarnished ministry.

Can God use imperfect people to reveal His glory? Uh, yeah, He has no other choice than to use imperfect people. However, we must be reminded that if we are in Christ, we are being built up in Him. Our ministry isn't what defines us, what Christ has done for us through the cross is what defines us. Our worth and identity is in Jesus. We are built in Him and He builds the church. It is from being connected to the Vine that the fruit of the ministry flows. It comes from our lives and should reflect His grace, His character and His love and ultimately produce good fruit.

The question to ask and answer is, "What type of fruit am I producing right now?" If you aren't seeing good fruit, if others aren't eating from the fruit that grows from your tree, if others aren't being edified around you or if there isn't evidence of the character of Christ and beauty of His heart in all that you do, it's time to stop and get reconnected to the Vine. Intimacy is about connection. Our relationship with God is built on intimacy. Nothing matters more than your personal connection to Jesus.

When we are connected to God daily, we WILL have a revelation of God through worship. This is why personal connection in worship is so important. In order to be fruitful and walk in everything God has designed for your life, you will need to cultivate a strong connection with God daily. This means spending time alone with God, learning to hear and discern His voice, reading His word daily, spending time in private worship and pursuing His presence and goodness. These are some of the ways we stay connected to the Vine. Ultimately, it is the Holy Spirit who leads us daily to stay connected to the Lord, we just need to learn to submit to His leading and not our own.

Study questions: CONNECTED TO THE VINE

What do you turn to when you feel drained and weak?

Do you find that leading worship feels like a heavy burden?

What are the specific things you do after you've led worship that help you stay in love with Jesus?

CHAPTER 3

THEOLOGIANS OF SONG

Just how important are the lyrics over the music?

Colossians 3:16 - Let the word of Christ dwell in you richly, teaching and admonishing one another in all wisdom, singing psalms and hymns and spiritual songs, with thankfulness in your hearts to God. (**ESV**)

I can still remember the song I heard when I walked into a church in South Florida; I can remember the energy, melody and even the lyrics. That's pretty crazy because I cannot, for the life of me, remember what the sermon was that day. Nor can I recall what the main points of the sermon were or what verses were read. Doesn't that scare you just a little bit? Week after week people go to churches all over the world to worship, pray and dive into God's Word with the fellowship of other believers. However, I am guessing the majority of Churchgoers would probably remember one or more of the songs with only a faint remembrance of the details of the message taught. Well, my friend, what this means for us who lead worship is that the songs we sing matter and they matter a LOT.

We are theologians of song; we are the preachers of the Word through melody and music. We minister the truth of God through psalms, hymns and spiritual songs. People remember in different ways, through interaction, through repetition and through visual illustrations. However, ideas put to music can be remembered for a lifetime. I remember jingles from my childhood that make this so true for me. I know every church has its own style and even its own feel for worship music but the core essential to what the body of Christ experiences is the same; connecting with God through songs and worship. God has given us the gift of music to help us remember truth.

Theology is the study of God and His attributes and perfections. To be a song theologian means that we are the ones who actually put long term, memorable and lasting ideas about God into people's hearts and minds. This takes place every weekend too. So, do lyrics of the songs we sing matter? Uh yes, big time! I have so many songs I can remember in my head right now from many years ago.

I can remember where I was when I heard the song, or perhaps the season of life I was in. For some reason God has given us an amazing gift in music which allows us to remember truths about life through music. I honestly believe that music is the one art form that transcends earth and heaven. It stimulates the mind, engages the heart, touches the soul and moves the body—God has given us a powerful gift in music. When Moses led and delivered God's people from Egypt, the first thing they did after crossing over the Red Sea was write a song about it... the Song of Moses.

When Christ was born, after centuries of silence, the heavens opened up and revealed all of heaven singing and declaring God's redemption through songs. When we look into the book of Revelation we see so many moments captured around singing, shouting, responding and declaring praises unto God and the Lamb that sits on the throne. This is why I believe the songs that we choose must be carefully chosen according to the content of their lyrics and message. Once we deliver them, if we deliver them with passion and excellence, they will become ideas and thoughts that will grow into the hearts and minds of God's people that will linger for a lifetime.

For this reason, I believe that the songs we sing and lead others in worship should be Christ-centered, presenting the gospel in a real and clear way. Lyrics need to magnify and declare who God is, what He has done, and what He will do. Our worship should exalt His nature and attributes, allowing God's people to realize His magnificence and glory. Worship should help lead people into an encounter with God, hopefully leading to spiritual transformation as they are caught up into the power of God's presence.

Leading songs in worship has weight to it, it's a calling, it's a Kingdom assignment in which we teach theology to the hearts and minds of those we lead. The Bible says that Jesus is the image of the invisible God; the radiance of His glory (**Col 1:15, Hebrews 1:3**). Jesus is the definitive expression of God to us. Therefore, in worship, the songs we sing should also reflect this truth with clarity, with conviction and passion. We should aim to have clear lyrical expressions so the church can grow in their understanding of who God is as revealed in Christ Jesus.

Lyrics that make use of nature, metaphors or other ways of expressing God's love are fine; they help expand our way of seeing the whole picture. However, they should not veil or mask what is clear in scripture about God. In fact, I do enjoy songs like that. I love creative lyrics that help the mind paint pictures but as ministers of God who are called to lead worship gatherings that inspire and move people in their walk with God, the songs we choose should reflect the most talked about, sung about and celebrated topic in all eternity- God revealed in Jesus.

Choosing the right song with the right lyric is the way we steward this calling as ministers of worship. Thinking deeply about each song's meaning, with caution and care, is what we should be doing every time we put a song list together. I can't think of a greater task than being entrusted by God and the local church to put ideas about

God in the hearts and minds of His people when they gather!

When I take a look at heaven in Scripture, I see a powerful worship gathering around the Lamb of God seated on the throne, exalting and magnifying Jesus. My heart's desire is to align my expression of worship as a leader to what is happening in heaven and release that on earth through the songs we sing.

Revelation 4: 9-11 (NASB) And when the living creatures give glory and honor and thanks to Him who sits on the throne, to Him who lives forever and ever, the twenty-four elders will fall down before Him who sits on the throne, and will worship Him who lives forever and ever, and will cast their crowns before the throne, saying, "Worthy are You, our Lord and our God, to receive glory and honor and power; for You created all things, and because of Your will they existed and were created."

Study questions: THEOLOGIANS OF SONG

What do you look for in a worship song?

Do you search the Father's heart in the scriptures for truth when selecting songs?

If each song you sang last week were put into a sermon, what would that sermon say about what God has done through Christ? Is the message of the gospel clear?

CHAPTER 4

OUR CREATIVE CRISIS

When leading worship, can creativity hurt or help others engage in worship?

Psalms 78:72 With unselfish devotion David became their shepherd. With skill he guided them. (**GWT**)

Have you ever ordered a product online? I recently purchased something for the house online. I looked through all of the pictures, checked the sizes and features, then I went and read through all of the reviews. After I did my research, I went ahead, clicked the button and ordered it. When it finally arrived I was excited, I grabbed my scissors and opened the box, began to unwrap that amazing and fun bubble paper until I saw... I saw.... wait. What is this? I checked the invoice to make sure it was the correct item but I was confused. The color and texture didn't match the description at all. I went back online just to be certain of what I had ordered. Well, you guessed it, I was disappointed to learn that what I thought I was getting wasn't what I got at all.

You know the level of disappointment that comes over you when you hope for something that you know you need but what you received didn't live up to the hype? Frustrating. When people decide to go to church they come expecting something. Most times they get invited by a friend or they watch online and they are normally persuaded to come because they have been told that they will love it. When they choose to come, they go with an idea about what church is or can be, especially if a friend invited them. If they come to attend a service once and they like it, they may decide to come back. If they choose to come back, they come back hoping to find what they liked about it in order to determine if it's something they want to become a part of.

We are creatures of habit. We love to follow patterns; in fact our brains thrive on learning patterns. Our brains help us understand our world by taking in information, processing that information and then sending signals to us to help us manage our day. The science behind it is compelling which is why I believe so strongly in creating some sort of consistency of expectations when it comes to corporate worship settings. Music and song are no different for us; we remember words and melodies that are "catchy", also known as a song "hook" for a reason. A song is an arrangement of notes, organized and categorized into a format or pattern so that it can be remembered, learned and hopefully loved. Corporate worship plays a major part in a person's choice of Christian fellowship.

As worship leaders, we play a role in their experience when visiting church and attending it normally. We are investing in their spiritual growth and formation through the songs and music we choose as leaders. We are also artists; we are creative thinkers. Here is where the rub begins. Genuine worship should remain the goal as we use creativity to enhance it. Let me explain this a little more so that the point isn't misunderstood. Creativity is from God and is needed in the church. We have already established that God has given us worship in order to find our purpose and align our perspective in Him. We are here to minister to the Lord and bless His people in His name. Therefore, the worship service isn't a platform to serve our inner creative hunger but a place where we help people encounter God with our creativity.

We are wired and inspired to innovate and keep things new and fresh. We get bored fast. God put that in us to express who He is through the arts. Scripture has a lot to say about keeping things new and fresh in our hearts. There are new seasons, new songs, new blessings and new movements. God is a God of new. This is what He does. He takes the old and makes things new. The new described in Scripture however doesn't necessarily mean something uncreated. It's more of a "keep it fresh" idea. Now, as creative people we love to change things up. We love to think outside the box and try different things and ways to express the arts. This is necessary and vital in the Kingdom of God. The arts are a powerful way to describe God's heart, mind and Word. However, creativity that doesn't have boundaries can also have a negative effect if we don't monitor it.

As leaders of worship, we are aiming to create unity and direct people's hearts towards God's heart through song. Being intentional, I have found, is the key to balancing this inner conflict of creativity versus consistency. We cultivate moments in our worship services to unify the body of Christ and the visitors towards a clear message about Christ and the gospel.

Honestly, my desire as a worship leader is to help lead the room in song and in moments where they can sing to God and receive from Him. The last thing I want to do is make that experience confusing by breaking the pattern in which they have connected with the song I am leading. This takes discernment, prayer and humility to ask God for His guidance on how to create fresh moments and still allow a consistent framework for the people of God to open their hearts, unveil themselves in the gaze of their Savior.

As creatively minded leaders, I believe we can move from old songs to new songs too rapidly. This also means that we can lose sight of how people engage with those songs depending on how quickly we introduce new ideas and songs. Changing and recreating comes easily to us. Songs we did two weeks ago are already old for us, especially after rehearsing it a bunch of times and singing it in numerous services. We spend so much time rehearsing the songs that it can get overly familiar to us much more quickly than for the people who attend our local church. What we need to remember is that not everyone can move at this pace of change.

The majority of people who go to church don't listen to the songs as often as we do. On the contrary, worship leaders put in a lot of time preparing for church services and in that process, a song can be heard and rehearsed many times over. This is where practicing discipline is needed. Engagement and corporate singing is a vital part of worship services. This isn't a man made idea, it's all over the scriptures as I mentioned at the start with Moses, through Christs' birth and in Revelation where we read the masses singing and praising together.

When people know the song, they sing from the heart and open up their hearts and engage in worship. When people don't know the song, they are more focused on learning and listening to follow along rather than releasing the praise in their heart. One of the most beautiful things about worship services to me is hearing the people of God sing together with one voice, opening up their hearts to God in song. When every heart becomes unified and is led to respond to the goodness of God, this is the goal in leading worship in my perspective. We help people encounter God by creating an environment where faith becomes alive, unity is manifested and our praise and worship is released unto God.

Our role as worship leaders serves a specific function in the local church. I believe that as worship leaders we have a creative need that has to be nurtured and we tend to force that need to be met through our worship leading settings. We unintentionally sacrifice engaging corporate worship moments for fresh creative expressions. In turn, there should be a healthy balance in which creativity serves the purpose of corporate worship.

We serve to help people connect with God in worship. I can't think of anything more powerful than walking into a church that is alive with praise, where hands are lifted, hearts are open and voices are singing to God. What a powerful way to evangelize. Cultivating an environment where God's people are invited and engaged in worship is the essence of leading worship. The people entrusted to you in your local church are precious to God. The gifts He has placed within you are for building up the church. The hard part for us is to learn how to submit our gifts to the service of others but it's in doing this that our gifts find their purpose, which is to glorify God and build up his church.

So, find ways to keep it fresh and simple. Be intentional about the whole experience, finding the right balance of creativity and consistency, so that when we lead worship we can help people know Christ through the songs that we sing. Ask the Lord for the right ideas. Ask the Holy Spirit to help you use your creativity to serve the mission of your church.

Take the risks that will help people engage their hearts and minds in your worship gatherings. A church that worships together and encounters God together will grow together and you are specifically called and equipped by God to help lead that journey in worship.

<u>Study questions</u>: OUR CREATIVE CRISIS

Where do you get fresh ideas for leading worship?

Behind every idea is a reason; what convictions drive your ideas?

When people leave your worship service, what do you hope impacts them the most?

CHAPTER 5

A SPIRIT OF EXCELLENCE

Pursuing excellence matters but what motivates our best efforts?

1 Corinthians 12:31 But earnestly desire the greater gifts. And I will show you a still more excellent way. (**ESV**)

I LOVE watching #SaltBAE. Do you know who he is? He is probably the most entertaining meat chef in the world. He puts so much style, passion, love, feeling and care into the meals he cooks. He has become a worldwide phenomenon because of it and has millions of Instagram followers. We always benefit from the love someone puts into their work because we can *feel* that love through their dedication. I believe that preparing to lead worship with excellence and preparing for excellence begins with the true understanding of these four letters L-O-V-E.

If you've ever attended a wedding you have probably heard someone read what is known as the Chapter of Love. What many may not know is that Paul was writing in the context of leadership and gifts in the church, not about relationships. Paul uses a term at the end of the previous chapter where he hints at "a more excellent way" of how to use our gifts in the Kingdom.

We also forget that Paul was a single man, so he wasn't blogging about relationships and love. He wasn't tweeting about how to obtain the perfect relationship. He was actually teaching the church about the uses and abuses of spiritual gifts in the church. Paul reveals to us that without the proper motivation behind the gifts, we fail miserably to have the proper impact. In other words, without love as the motive, the effort is null and void. What we believe and feel on the inside is expressed on the outside.

You see, the motive behind the action matters more than the action itself. People are often impressed with gifts and talents but God looks at the heart and the character of the person. Who we become matters more to God than what we accomplish. How we accomplish what we do in ministry matters more than what we accomplish. Let me translate if I may... If it does not have love, it doesn't count. God measures our growth according to how we love, not according to what we know.

Paul, in describing how the spiritual gifts fit together, steps into the topic of love with a clear outline of what love looks like. He explains line by line, or more like a punch after punch, what real love looks like. He describes a love that is superior to any human love, a love that sees beyond the failures and flaws of a person. It's a love so intense, filled with grace and a commitment to care and protect us while never losing interest or strength for us. Paul in essence is describing the heart of God to us. God IS love. When God's love is at work within us, how we use our gifts takes on a different approach. Human effort devoid of love misses the mark because what makes something excellent is the love that inspired it. Excellence is always a result of L-O-V-E.

Paul says in Scripture that love is the more excellent way of serving. Being rooted in love impacts the fruit we produce. We all want to leave a legacy that impacts the Kingdom but we cannot ignore what our motivation for doing so looks like. Let me make a clear statement here; mere human effort alone doesn't equate to worship that pleases God. God has outlined worship for us and it doesn't come on our terms no matter how hard we try in our effort and strength.

Worship must be rooted in Christ in order for it to be an offering of praise that pleases God. To be clear on this point, without the atonement of Christ, anything we do, even at our best human effort falls short because no one comes to the Father except through Jesus. Human effort is required in order to achieve excellence but I just wanted to be sure to remind us that mere human effort alone is not the goal in leading worship, pointing people towards Christ is.

In order to point people towards Christ, we need the power and help of the Holy Spirit. When we are pointing people towards Christ, we want our efforts to be motivated and rooted in His love. Since we have established that worship is a response to God, we receive that revelation, we respond with L-OV-E in all we do, we respond with worship. Let me say it this way, when I finally see His love for me, I'm inspired to respond with my best. Love begets love.

Excellence is about love and about being good stewards of what God has entrusted to us. God has given us ability, talent and a calling and we are responsible for how we steward those. Excellence may look differently from time to time because it is a moving target. It is something we pursue. This is why it requires us putting in the work every time. It demands a high level of engagement and effort. When someone finds joy and love in what they do we see a spirit of excellence in action. We see excitement and passion. We also see a heart engaged with its work revealed to us as artistry.

A spirit of excellence desires to constantly grow and improve because it's motivated by love. When you love what you do and why you do it, you most naturally give your best. Excellence is a fruit of love. Love is the more excellent way of using our gifts in the Kingdom.

Now, let's unpack excellence in regards to leading worship. Excellence requires mental and emotional engagement. It also requires training and a personal commitment to growth. Excellence is the result of developed and matured skill.

Again, as worship leaders we aren't just seeking to give our best human effort, but rather we are trying to make sure that the motive of our hearts is rooted in God's love and that love is the motive that inspires our best efforts. The emphasis here isn't just in the development of skill but the inner working of God's love as evidenced in the use of those skills and gifts.

I define excellence this way: **giving our best effort without being a distraction**. If it was without distraction but I held back from giving my best effort, it isn't excellence. On the other hand, if I gave my best effort but it was distracting, then I need more training. Love isn't lazy. Love isn't afraid. Love isn't passive. Love takes action and it's expressed through devotion and commitment. Excellence says, we don't lean on yesterday's results; we put in our best work every time. Ultimately, for me to cultivate a spirit of excellence I need to be motivated by love and also have the proper training to do it.

It's also important to note that having a safe environment is vital to pursuing excellence. Perfect love casts out fear. An environment of punishment and fear will choke a true spirit of excellence. Mistakes will be made and mental errors will occur; what we want to monitor is the root cause of these. We are responsible and accountable for what God has commissioned us to do. Here is the question we should be asking: Is the root cause a lack of training or lack of engagement? Excellence will require both training and engagement. Excellence is also personal. It isn't something that happens unintentionally. It requires everyone to commit and pursue it together. It's important for us to remember that we pursue God's purpose with excellence from a place of acceptance in Christ. Our motive must be a love that is complete.

I have to make this point clear because as I stated earlier, the motive of our hearts play a huge role here. If you don't believe you are accepted by God you will strive to be accepted in your performance to God. If you don't believe that the perfection and righteousness of Christ is upon you, you will be motivated to earn that acceptance in everything you do for God. You will fall for the trap in believing God loves you because of your best effort. Beloved, let's remember that God loves us because we are in Christ and love is WHO He is. Greater yet still, God has already demonstrated His great love for us on the cross.

Here are a few things to consider when cultivating a spirit of excellence for your team. The vision should be clear. The standards should be taught and shared often. Along with clarity of vision and standards should come training and development. It is our responsibility to help develop and equip God's people, helping them grow into their calling. No one becomes great at what they do by themselves. Everyone needs to be coached and trained and that includes us as well.

I'll share some of my struggles here. I come from a professional background in the music industry and was used to performing at a high level in order to be successful. Every opportunity meant not only giving my best, it also meant I might not get another opportunity. I went after music with all I had, gave it my very best because I loved it. After coming to Christ, the struggle was real for me. When God called me into leading worship I simply didn't know the difference between performing and leading worship. I believed that God was more pleased with me because of how hard I was working. It always had to be perfect, it always had to be great, it always had to be right.

My motive was to gain God's approval through my pursuit of excellence, instead of realizing that in Christ I already had it. One day, while in prayer and worship God revealed something to me that changed my life. God spoke to me and said that His affection for me had nothing to do with what I did. I didn't understand the gospel up until that point. Who I was and what I did was not the same thing.

Furthermore, my relationship with God wasn't based on how well I did it. I've come to understand that God is surrounded day and night by perfection and true excellence in worship. Heaven has perfect music. Yet, here I was, thinking, God should stop what's going on in heaven and check me out because He would be so impressed with me, or so I thought. I realized that my standing with God is not defined by my work for God. Rather, my standing with God is defined by His love for me. God loves me because that is who He is.

That day in prayer God set me free from that religious and performance spirit. His grace came in like a flood and swept me into a deep place of love and acceptance in Him. I have been free ever since. Now, whenever I lead worship I can honestly say I am completely motivated by His great love for me and I respond in love to Him. Excellence in our worship gatherings is important but it cannot be devoid of love. Love is why we do what we do. We do all things in response to all He has done for us.

So, we keep our love on at all times. Leading worship is demanding of our time, our focus and our talent but we must stay grounded in L-O-V-E. When we prepare, when we execute and when we try to figure out how to make things better it's because of L-O-V-E. We constantly look for ways to improve as we pursue excellence through the lens of love. L-O-V-E is the only thing by which we will be measured in eternity. We remember that love is our motive, not fear. We are inspired by faith, not discouraged by failure. We learn and we grow. We focus on His perfection instead of focusing on our performance knowing that we are accepted in the beloved and we are becoming all He has created us to be. Saved by love to become love.

Study questions: A SPIRIT OF EXCELLENCE

What is the attitude of your team when it comes to preparation?

How do you measure the love your team has for one another when they serve together?

Is preparing for worship and leading worship a fun experience for you and your team?

CHAPTER 6

REST ROOM

Matthew 11:28 Then Jesus said, "Come to me, all of you who are weary and carry heavy burdens, and I will give you rest. (**NLT**)

I once drove from Rhode Island to Brooklyn overnight with my friend to help him move his stuff to Providence. Now, I didn't know he was making the move, he sort of showed up to my house late and crashed and asked me if I could drive back with him to pick up the rest of his stuff. Since I didn't have anything going on the next day I said yes. The plan was to sleep a little, then head South on I95 around 3am. The alarm woke me up, we got ready and since he asked if I could drive first (it was about a 3 hour ride) I hopped into the moving truck and off we went. As we began to enter Connecticut I looked at the fuel level and saw that it was below empty!

I was widening my eyes because I didn't even think to look at the fuel before we left. I woke him up and asked him if he had filled the truck with gas... he said he forgot. "You forgot?!" Then as I'm in the left lane I could feel the gas pedal pulsing and the truck slowing down. By now we are WIDE awake and realizing we've run out of fuel. We need to pull over to figure this out. We completely ran out of gas, had to walk 3 miles to get some gas, walk it back, pour it in and after we lost three hours finally got the truck started again, then decided to get more gas before getting back on the highway.

How does a moment in life become so cluttered? Something so simple can become very stressful when we are faced with making choices with little rest. Tiredness is always a recipe for danger. I wonder how many of us have been leading worship week after week without taking time to recover from it. We can often forget that what we do is spiritual warfare.

We stand in the gap to proclaim the good news of God over the darkness that blinds people from seeing the glory of God in Christ. Spiritual warfare can be difficult to quantify. It's a battle that cannot be measured in the natural realm. Not only does it require a high level of spiritual engagement, but it also requires a high level of emotional engagement. This urgency and intensity can often be overlooked and can be a silent ministry assassin for worship leaders. Leading worship is a spiritual battle.

Paul states in **2 Corinthians 4:4** "Satan, who is the god of this world, has blinded the minds of those who don't believe. They are unable to see the glorious light of the Good News. They don't understand this message about the glory of Christ, who is the exact likeness of God." I want you to consider this thought; the enemy has a goal to keep people from seeing God's glory. How do you think he feels about you helping people see that glory through worship and praise? Our enemy is not going to sit back and do nothing.

This is why we put on the mighty armor of God and step out in faith. In His grace and power, God has given us authority to declare the praises of His grace with boldness and passion. This requires an incredible amount of spiritual activity that flows from our souls and when left unchecked can become dangerous.

Every week we are building people up, equipping, teaching and mentoring. Ministry work is never done; we can easily fall into the temptation of working all of the time. I know of too many leaders in ministry who choose to skip rest or recovery time because they feel the weight of the ministry demands. Beloved, Jesus said His burden is light and His yoke is easy. Let us not forget that we are to cast our cares on Him because He cares for us. Without being intentional about rest, you will dry up and wood that is dry burns the fastest. There are a number of dangers that await us when we choose not to rest. Rest is a gift from God and we can choose to enter into it, or we can choose to ignore it.

The burden of leadership is responsibility but it is a yoke sustained in the grace of God. The burdens of the people belong to the Lord. Some of these dangers stem from getting our identity from ministry. We begin to find our value and worth from what we do. Another danger from not resting is that fear begins to fill our hearts instead of faith. We begin to think we need to be in control of everything, do everything, plan everything or we need to be involved in everything.

Instead of creating a culture of empowerment, we create a culture of control. We become convinced that the success of the ministry revolves around us. We begin to believe " the team isn't going to make it without me." We want to be at every meeting, part of every decision and all of these come from fear, which again is rooted from identity issues. Another danger is that without rest, we never allow anyone else to step into their calling.

We can become a roadblock to someone else's growth. Instead of training, teaching and leading, we are the one doing everything. The core of ministry work is equipping and allowing other leaders to step up and find their purpose. Exhaustion in ministry is all too common and sad, causing most in ministry to lose their joy in serving others which in turn leads to destructive patterns that harm valuable relationships. For some, marriages and families have completely fallen apart due to the demands of ministry.

Losing sight of rest leads to poor choices, clouded thinking, bad habits and then we turn to coping behaviors. Darkness moves strongest when we are at our weakest. The issue to monitor here is pride. Why are we not resting? What is at the root of our restlessness? A friend once coached me and said that we all have an occupation that keeps us working but it's our preoccupation that keeps us busy.

Don't allow busyness to corrupt your fruitfulness. What does making room for rest look like to you? For me, it starts and remains with connecting and abiding in Christ. We find rest for our souls in Jesus... not in ministry or ministry activity. We are saved to belong to God not saved to work for God. We stay rooted in His love and He keeps us from stumbling. We hustle because what we do matters but we don't stress. We take ground but we don't push. We work hard but we remain tender hearted.

There is a sense of urgency in everything we do and a greater sense of importance but only God causes things to grow. God saved us to become worshipers. We are children of God, not employees of religion. Jesus is our resting place and we work from resting in Him. He calls us and He sustains us.

An easy way to measure where you are in this area is to monitor your joy level. Are you easily irritated? Does change really mess you up? Are you more often filled with fear and anxiety instead of excitement and faith? These are the surface signs that your soul is weary and needs to be recalibrated by the rest that only the Presence of God can bring because remember; in His presence there is fullness of Joy (**Psalm 16:11**).

At the root of avoiding rest is a doubting and unbelieving heart. The truth is, it takes faith to rest. It takes faith to step away and empower someone else to lead the team. It takes faith to understand that ministry is not dependent on us. It takes faith to do all of those things and we know that without faith it is impossible to please God.

Leading worship is demanding on the mind, will and emotions. If you want a healthy ministry and you want to see the fruit of your labor grow in a healthy way, create room to rest in Christ. Find time to relax and have fun, get removed from the work and allow Jesus to restore your soul. Receive His love. Abide in His grace. Practice the discipline of His daily presence. Remembering that a restful heart produces healthy choices, actions and results. Jesus invites us to come to Him and find rest, rest for the soul which can only be satisfied in Him.

Study questions: REST ROOM

Do you have healthy boundaries to keep your soul healthy?

Are you being productive or just busy?

Do you find it hard to say no?

CHAPTER 7

GROWING PAINS

Psalm 119:71 It was good for me to suffer, so that I might learn your statutes. (**NET**)

Pain in ministry is a tough topic to bring up. Pain is also very evident in all of scripture. I have walked through many painful seasons of ministry, which is why I want to be sensitive about this topic but still address it. If you've served as a worship leader in ministry I am certain that pain is part of your journey. If you are considering becoming a worship leader this is a topic we need to cover. Depending on what part of the world you grew up in your theology of suffering and the reality of pain might look very different than mine. I was born and raised in the Bronx, NY, in a lower class family. I walked to school everyday, rain or shine, summer or winter. As a teenager I took subways and City buses back and forth from school. Although in America this would be classified as a lower class income family, try and compare that to families who don't have any transportation at all and are just wondering what they will eat to survive today. It's all perspective right?

Think about how many times perhaps you and I have become frustrated because we didn't know where we wanted to go eat for lunch in comparison to people who just don't have food at all. Our life experiences can strongly shape our reality and in a sense cause us to process discomfort as pain and suffering, when it really isn't. Suffering is a topic in Scripture that we cannot avoid addressing or reading about. It's a topic that can become very distorted because of our upbringing. I don't want to address the *theology* of suffering in ministry, however, I want to address the *topic* of pain in ministry because it does happen and very well may happen to you.

When we gave our lives to Christ and became saved, we became part of God's family and enlisted into the ministry of His Kingdom. If you are saved that means you are also called, if you are called that means you are in full time ministry. Full-time ministry does not mean you work for a church, it simply means you are part of the kingdom of God and have a calling and purpose for your life. You may not be employed by a church, but everyone who belongs to Jesus is called to ministry.

Everyone who belongs to Jesus is part of the Kingdom and has been called to serve. Everyone is a minister and a Royal Priest. In ministry one thing can be expected, you will be required to grow and growth always involves some sort of pain. Ministry is about people, serving people, working with people, reporting to people, supporting people, praying for people and people are, well, not perfect.

We are broken vessels. Add to this reality experiences with leaders and pastors and now you've got a really complicated situation that can sometimes produce hurt and wounds in the soul that take a long time to heal. Some of the deepest areas of pain I've suffered was from leaders I served with and for. People are human and humans aren't perfect, unfortunately that does include you and me. God puts His incredible purpose into broken vessels. He does this to demonstrate His power and grace in our lives. Let me be clear, everything that happens in ministry or in a church is not the way God planned for it to be.

There is the will of man and the will of God. Sometimes God allows the will of man to move forward in His sovereignty and sometimes the will of man surrenders to the will of God. God knows the end from the beginning and this is where we place our trust and hope in Him and His purpose. Getting hurt in ministry is painful and can come as a shock. This is because we expect things to be different behind the "walls" of a church. When in reality, as a friend of mine says, when you look behind the veil you will discover that it can be dark, dirty and messy. Churches are not perfect. In fact, every time I thought I found one it changed the moment I got there.

No matter how many times I've tried to move around to avoid pain, one thing I always took with me was my own messiness. The good news is that Jesus came to make all things new, including our messiness. Through the power of His Spirit He washes and renews us into something wonderful and glorious. Our job is to yield and surrender to His leading and healing. We get to participate in His prompting and ultimately allow the Spirit to complete His work of sanctification in our lives. We can live in freedom.

What we must be watchful for is a root of bitterness. Bitterness is the result of a wound that never heals. You can't see bitterness right away. Bitterness grows in the dark parts of our soul. We spin the situation over and over in our heads and the enemy adds fuel to the fire, filling our minds with negative thoughts. We tend to relive the situation again and again, carrying it around in our hearts until it finally breaks the soil and begins to manifest. When we don't allow God to heal us, anger sets in.

Bitterness is unhealed pain that begins to spring up with anger, resentment, sarcasm, gossip and slander. These are just some of the sins that are birthed when we don't let God deal with bitterness early on. Pain is not without purpose. Joseph suffered pain. Job suffered pain. David suffered pain. Paul suffered pain. Peter suffered pain. Jesus suffered pain. We live in a world that is full of pain but also full of life. People often confuse pain with harm.

I'll give you an example. One of my kids had a tooth that was loose and it needed to come out. They were so afraid of the pain they would feel and horrified by the blood that would come gushing out (this is how they viewed it), they kept avoiding it. Would there be pain? Yes. Would the removal of the tooth harm them? No. Pain in ministry is an unfortunate result of our old sinful nature. Jesus came to set us free and it takes time for us to learn to walk in that freedom. However, how we choose to respond to pain is up to us.

God can use every situation to develop and mature our character for His glory. God can redeem every chapter of pain in our story. When we get wounded we must learn to run to the cross and surrender it to Jesus. Pain can be used to reveal something in us that hasn't died on the cross. God is a master surgeon; He knows exactly where to drive the nail.

Sometimes pain can teach us something we aren't willing to learn about ourselves. God is always developing our character. In fact, whenever God gives us a cross to bear, it's not to harm us; it's to transform us. Pain, when surrendered to God, can help us grow and mature, and ultimately lead us to authenticity and purity in our worship. The deeper the pain, the stronger the praise.

God's Word tells us that He disciplines the ones He loves. Just think about that... if He didn't love us, He would choose to leave us alone to our sinful devices. God has an incredible plan for us but in order to walk in that plan we must allow maturity to take place in us so that He can flow through us. Growing up hurts sometimes. The good news is that God loves His children too much to leave them where they are, even if it hurts. He never intends to harm us, but rather heal us, develop us and mature us into the fullness of Christ.

Yes, there is pain in ministry and sometimes it's hard to understand it all, especially when we are going through it. But God loves, heals, guides and restores all things in His purpose and plan. No one suffered more than Jesus on the cross and that is why we can be sure God understands our pain. At times we will feel ignored, torn down and discarded. Growth in ministry will produce pain and hurt because we are only human.

Beloved, let me encourage you to never allow ministry pain to grow into bitterness. Instead, give God your pain and trust Him in the process. God always has a purpose beyond our understanding and He allows us to mature through experiences to reveal that purpose in eternity.

Here on Earth, things aren't supposed to be perfect and the church is filled with imperfect people. Yet, God still restores and heals. If we can hang in there and allow God to clean up the mess in us, we will see His grace at work through us. Then when we enter into eternity, we will finally be able to see His purpose for us in Him.

Study questions: GROWING PAINS

How do you respond when you feel offended?

How are you getting coached and receiving feedback?

How do you process seasons of personal growth?

CHAPTER 8

FEAR OF MAN IS A TRAP

Criticism and praise: How can we avoid the lure of what people think of us?

Galatians 1:10 Obviously, I'm not trying to win the approval of people, but of God. If pleasing people were my goal, I would not be Christ's servant. (**NLT**)

Do you remember what happened to Peter on the night that Jesus was taken into custody by the Pharisees to be judged and crucified? He followed Jesus to see what was going to happen to him but in the process, a person in the courtyard recognized his face and confronted him as a follower of Jesus. It was in that moment that the fear of man got ahold of Peter in such a strong way that it led him to deny Jesus three times, just as Jesus said he would. Maybe you remember another incident with Peter in the book of Acts where Paul came to visit and had to confront Peter because he wasn't demonstrating the full power of a gospel-centered life in front of his friends. Paul called him out because he was treating the Gentiles differently than his own people. Again, here was the fear of man influencing Peter.

Peter loved people. Peter also loved what they thought about him. He loved how they perceived him so much that it influenced what he said and did. In these two examples we see a clear warning for us. We see that wanting to be accepted and approved by people is a trap that can lead us away from being properly aligned with Christ and the gospel. Let me dig deeper here if I can.

The true power of the gospel is that I am accepted in Christ and my acceptance is not based on my performance as a believer but rather I am saved by grace through faith in Christ's performance as a savior. The emphasis is IN Christ. His righteousness has been imputed to me, my sin and unrighteousness was imputed to Him. This is the great exchange, "He who knew no sin, became sin so that we might become the righteousness of God in Christ" (**1 Corinthians 5:21**).

When we really believe the good news in our hearts, the gospel finally sets us free. We become free to accept the reality that we are not perfect. The pressure to be perfect or pretend is lifted from us. I know I have issues and blind spots and I also know in Christ I have been perfected. Since I am now accepted in Christ, I can grow and learn freely. I am free to love others and free to serve without the lure of people's approval or without the temptation of people's opinion of me.

What does this have to do with leading worship? If your identity isn't rooted in Christ, you will make your ministry your identity. When your heart becomes anchored in your ministry, you develop an unhealthy response to what people think of you. Without being anchored in the gospel, you will be easily swayed and tossed by the masses. The praise of people will entice you and the criticism of people will crush you. Remember beloved, we minister to God, to an audience of One.

I have personally seen God work in this. There was a time when I was leading worship and some people were not happy with the new thing God was doing. I was seeking the face of God in this season, I was in prayer and fasting, I was serving with love and humility. Even with all of that, the enemy still found ways to discourage me, strike fear into my thoughts and tried to get me to stop and back down. People began to voice their discontent through emails, asking why things were changing and shifting. As this started I could feel God say, "keep going, I am with you, believe, trust in me." The real myth here is that if I do what pleases people they will finally love me. We all know that really isn't true. Half the time I don't even understand my own heart, how could I possibly know what I want?

God knows what I want and more importantly He knows what I need. When fear begins to attack us and when we become too attentive to what people are saying, we risk missing what God is saying. We must always keep coming back to God in prayer and ask what is God doing? What is His heart? If we don't, fear will intimidate us and we will end up listening to a few unhappy people and give them the loudest voice in our lives and ministry. People will always have their own preferences, opinions, thoughts and feelings on worship. People have opinions on the style, the expression, the volume or even the presentation.

Believe me, you will never win consensus. That is not what worship is supposed to be focused on anyway because God calls us to serve and minister to Him. Worship is always unto the Lord and as long as you are genuinely seeking the Lord, serving the Lord with humility, living a life of grace and love, and living according to His heart for your life, He will cover you and He will bless the fruit of your labor. There are things to work on and improve and likely even change, but it all flows from the heart of God and His purpose. There will be temptations to fold under the fear of what people think. More importantly what people think about us can become an even greater temptation.

Being considerate of others and being thoughtful is the right approach to this. Take time to listen to people and really hear their heart, as this is one of the best ways to stay humble and loving. Beyond that, you must trust in what God is leading you to do under the direction and leadership of your pastor.

As the ministers of music, go into the secret place with God, open His word and be reminded of what God thinks of you. If you are going to be in ministry or leadership you can't be effective if you are easily influenced by what people think. Try not to be lured down that road by staying at the foot of the cross and engaged daily in worship and the Word.

Always start by seeking the heart of the Father. As we seek His heart and minister unto Him, He imparts to us the wisdom and direction for what we do in ministry. God loves people and God wants His people to engage in worship. As spiritual leaders we do not ignore the people but rather, we focus on God's heart and as servants we seek His purpose for His people through ministry. Fear of man is a very real challenge in public ministry and it's a real part of worship ministry.

I love what Pastor Craig Groeschel says, "Becoming obsessed with what PEOPLE think about you is the quickest way to forget what GOD thinks about you."[6] I think that is the key... am I focused on what people think about me? Will they love me and accept me? Will they like me because of this? Am I doing a good enough job for them?

We have to remember to stay connected to Jesus and get our affirmation and approval from Him daily. Ministry is not about what people think; it's about loving them enough to give them what they need. This takes both humility and courage.

When it comes to leading worship, we guard our hearts and walk in a manner worthy of the calling. We keep our focus on what God has declared about us in His word, this is what really matters. If your heart is focused on Christ and your life is surrendered to Him, He will bless the labor of your work and He will guide you. The evidence of His grace will be upon you and He will bless what He has called you to do.

So, don't worry about the approval of people. Walk in grace, live in love, be humble, be a servant. Remember that you are accepted by God in Christ and remember what God's Word says, "For God has not given us a spirit of fear, but of power and of love and of a sound mind" (**1 Timothy 1:7 NKJV**).

Study questions: FEAR OF MAN IS A TRAP

Does the opinion of people have an extreme affect on you?

Do you feel freedom when leading worship or is it fear based?

How often are you getting fresh revelation from God's heart for direction in worship?

CHAPTER 9

SERVANT LEADERSHIP

Can a servant be a leader? Can a leader be a servant?

Romans 12:8 If your gift is to encourage others, be encouraging. If it is giving, give generously. If God has given you leadership ability, take the responsibility seriously. And if you have a gift for showing kindness to others, do it gladly. (**NLT**)

The bible often refers to God's people as sheep. I have never taken care of a real flock of sheep but from what I can see it takes a lot of attentive and careful management. Sheep flock together when given direction but they also tend to drift away at times when discarded or left unattended. The Bible also uses the term shepherd when referring to leaders in ministry. For many leaders, they can get confused about the whole servant leadership thing. Here is what I know; you can ride horses and you can drive cattle but sheep are to be shepherded. This lesson alone took me years to understand. Jesus came to model this for us as the Good Shepherd. Since leadership can be a complex subject, I just want us to focus on the impact it has when it comes to developing people. After all, leadership is about working with people, caring for people and assembling the gifts and talents of people for the common purpose of a vision.

This is how I define leadership; **leadership at its core is about advancing the mission by developing**

people and making those around you great. The question is how do we go about doing this? Do we drive people, make demands, order and push those we lead in order to get results? Or do we serve them? I believe that Godly leadership is rooted in having the heart of a servant. Jesus came to serve, not to be served. However, this can become a very vague idea and before you know it, instead of leaders leading, there can be a passivity that creates confusion.

Leadership is a clear spiritual gift in scripture and calling given from the Lord. These two ideas, being a servant and being a leader, are not opposed to one another.

Simon Sinek has a brilliant thought on this; he says, "Leadership is not about being in charge, leadership is about caring for those in your charge."[4] A leader who cares for those they lead is a servant leader. Here are some ways I can best describe this. Servant leaders consider their teams with every decision they make because they want to serve them well and help them succeed. Servant leaders invite insight and input from the stakeholders involved in the decisions. They cultivate a healthy culture where voices are heard. A servant leader is always thinking about how things will impact the team. Servant leaders know that great things happen because of great people. Brilliant people are what make things work. Servant leaders love those they lead and always lead with love.

Telling people what to do doesn't require leadership skills. Anyone can be a boss. Forcing people to respond to demands or creating an environment of punishment isn't leadership at all. As worship leaders we are to shepherd those in our care. What I'm *not* saying here is that creating accountability and boundaries are bad, not at all, to the contrary. Accountability is part of trusting being on a team and so are boundaries because everyone is there to serve the mission and vision.

What I am trying to say is that if things are always stressful, there may be fear involved if everyone is trying to make the leader happy... it slows down the growth and empowerment of the team. A servant leader culture looks differently in the sense that servant leaders lead and serve their teams and those teams serve each other and the vision.

It is critical that our leadership is in alignment with the character and nature of who Jesus is. Jesus was the full embodiment of grace and truth. Servant leadership is rooted in faith, not fear. It is founded in trust, not control. Empowering others versus holding on to power. Our identity isn't rooted in being the leader, it is rooted in Christ. When we realize this, we are willing to lay down our titles and pick up our aprons to serve others.

Servant leaders desire to gain insight from those around them because they believe they can learn from anyone. They aren't trying to be the smartest person in the room. They are seeking to find the smartest person on their team. No task is ever beneath them because they esteem others greater than themselves. They are constantly teaching, emphasizing the why before the what. They are always learning and growing on a personal level. They are mutually submitted to their team. Although they have authority over certain areas they understand that they do not have the proper competency in every area. They are secure and they know that wisdom comes from a multitude of counsel. They understand that although they will make the final decision, they do not have to make every decision alone.

Servant leadership isn't the absence of leadership; it's leadership that always starts with a servant's heart. It has the attitude of humility. There are times when they must lead by example. There are moments when passion for purpose needs to be seen. Servant leaders never tell others to go the way without showing them the way first.

Servant leadership always starts with others in mind. It begins with looking ahead and staying above the details so the vision remains clear, making the win visible to those they serve. A servant leader is close enough to the action to feel the movement but high enough to see where things are headed. This is what servant leadership is about. Understanding that people are not a means to an end. Servant leaders explain why things change in order to help others process those changes. It's teaching others where they can win and showing them how to do it well. It's empowering those around them to advance the mission with their gifts.

A leader's true value isn't in the answers they give but in the questions they ask. Servant leaders listen much more than they speak. Servant leaders create safety for healthy debate because they know that when people finally understand something clearly, they devote themselves fully. In my walk with the Lord, I have discovered that He never pushes me, drives me, forces me or manipulates me. He leads me, lures me, guides me, teaches me and shows me things everyday. This is the heart of the Father for us as leaders.

Leadership isn't power, authority or being in charge... These are all myths. Leadership is about serving. Leadership is a calling that puts us outside of our comfort zone and allows us to become part of something bigger than ourselves. There is no higher calling than being a servant. Leaders should understand that their leadership giftings aren't for their own gain but rather they are for the benefit of those they serve. Although a person may have a title, the titles don't make them a leader, much less a servant leader.

Let's be honest, being called a servant isn't a glamorous title in our culture. But in the Kingdom of God it's the highest bestowed honor we could ever be given. Why? Jesus came to serve not to be served, so we follow His lead, His example and we serve those we are in charge of with love and care. Jesus is our greatest example of servant leadership. There is nothing more needed today in our ministries than humble leaders who serve the vision with care, love and integrity of heart.

Study questions: SERVANT LEADERSHIP

Do you desire to be in charge or are you more concerned about caring for those in your charge?

Would your team say that you are known for empowering others?

Does your worship ministry shine on your accomplishments and talents or does it shine a light on the leaders you serve?

CHAPTER 10

THE MISSION IS PEOPLE

Execution vs. Relationships - What matters more?

Ephesians 4:12 For the equipping of the saints and the building up of the body of Christ; (**NASB**)

Now that we have explored the truths of leading worship on a practical level, I want to take a moment to cover the most important part of being a worship leader. Loving people. The gifts, talents, experience, expertise, vision, ideas, passion and callings God gives us, isn't for us. Everything God puts in us is to love and edify His people. Every good and perfect gift entrusted to us is for the benefit and building up of God's people.

Ministry isn't about us; it's about people. People are remarkable, they are resilient, they are capable of doing amazing things and they have callings on their lives too. People are human. People are difficult. People have issues and people are just like us. When it comes to leading worship, you will discover that it requires the unity and effort of people. This is how it was in the Old Testament too. The Ark of the Covenant could not be transported by one person but was to be carried upon the shoulders of many. Coincidently, as worship leaders, God did not place us in a position of influence for our own advancement, but rather for the advancement of the kingdom of God.

To be human is to be flawed. Trust me, I have a lot and with that comes a variety of potential hazards and challenges. However, ministry is God's pathway for people to grow spiritually and to discover who He is through serving others. I look at it this way, we never use people to build ministry, we use ministry to build people. A worship leader's primary job is to develop people spiritually, not just musically. A leader's job isn't to generate more followers, it's to develop other leaders.

A healthy culture of leadership will have strong relationships, an environment of trust, a desire for growth and accountability towards the goals and vision of that team. Every great ministry team will have the right mixture of mission and relationships at work. Worship ministry teams require both talent and character. It's unique in the sense that it requires developed skills that impact others.

Therefore, standards are necessary and have to be communicated and met in order for it to produce fruit. The scriptures make it clear that our primary role is to equip the saints for ministry. Essentially what that means is that we use ministry to develop people spiritually. The mission isn't something that is detached from the call of caring for people - the mission IS people.

Ministry is about people. Many might label this differently but at its core it is discipleship. We develop people. That is the mission. Some leaders may be more bent towards relational connecting while others may be more focused on the execution of the mission. Neither of these is wrong or right, they are just different and how God designed us to function as a body. What I will say is that healthy teams are built on both. In order to accomplish the mission, the right people are required.

Dr. Henry Cloud, who has written a number of amazing books, uses a phrase "the wake we leave behind"[5] to describe the trail of impact that comes from our leadership style. We all get to look behind us and see the impact we are having in both the mission and the people we lead. Some leaders are so overly focused on the results that they leave a trail of wounded, hurt, abused and used people behind. Passion and drive are important but should never become more important than the love and care of people. For anyone who is task oriented you know #TheStruggleIsReal.

The mission and vision of a church is very important and God will hold us accountable to the things He entrusted us to do but everything we do should be rooted and motivated by love. On the other hand, some leaders are more relationally focused. This is wonderful, the ability to connect with people is a huge gift in leadership but if there are no boundaries it can create a culture where there isn't any urgency or accountability. There can even be a lack of focus or a failure to confront sometimes. It can become a place that is friendly and fun but not much is getting done.

The idea here isn't to choose one over the other. Like I said earlier, neither of these is wrong. In order to be successful in creating a culture of growth and a community of healthy worshipers, you will need to have both- a missional and relational focus. This is why developing leaders is so important in the long-term health and vision of a ministry. You won't have all of the gifts or all of the right filters to serve people. As a worship leader, it will be important for you to identify, develop and place leaders around you that can help you carry out the mission God has called you to. The truth is with the right mixture of mission focus and relational connecting, your worship team can grow into a healthy thriving community. Be careful of allowing the pressure of the mission to drown out the need for relational connection.

People long to be a part of something amazing and if you can keep this in view, you will have a fruitful and healthy worship ministry team. Being successful in your mission will require training, teaching, coaching and mentoring. It will require clear communication, goals, values and a commitment to excellence. Being successful in your relational community will require fellowship, marginal time to hang out, time for celebration, honor, personal connection, fun interactions and corporate times to gather and share.

As worship leaders, we have the most amazing opportunity to point people to Christ through song and praise. We also have the responsibility to help people grow in their calling as believers when they serve in our ministry teams. This is why we keep Jesus at the center of it all. It's when we see the heart of God clearly that we begin to serve others well. Jesus died for people, not a mission statement.

The mission IS ultimately about people. In order to accomplish the call of God on your life, you will need the right people with you. If you will position yourself in humility to be led daily by God's grace on how to do that, God will bless the fruit of your labor, leading you to create a healthy culture, a fruitful culture, a mature culture that can accomplish the mission, while enjoying the blessing of healthy relationships along the way.

Study questions: THE MISSION IS PEOPLE

Is the culture of your teams focused and/or fun?

Are you using ministry to build people or are you using people to build ministry?

How do you measure the balance of pursuing the vision of your team versus the health and care of your team?

Conclusion and encouragement

Thank you for taking the time to process each of these simple truths. I do pray we have been able to debunk many of the myths that we face as worship leaders. I also hope this helps guide you and equip you to serve your calling well. I hope you found them insightful, challenging, inspiring and maybe even a little uncomfortable. What you do matters but who you are matters even more.

Leading worship is not a simple call; it requires the proper mixture of passion for the Lord with the desire to equip the saints of the church. Both heart and skill must come together in order for it to work as God designed it in worship.

In the Old Testament it was very clear that anyone chosen to lead worship had to be a skilled person. David was chosen to minister in the palace for Saul because he was known as a skilled musician, but the heart cannot be overlooked in the process. Our character must be humble, contrite and tender before God. We are saved to be children of God, who out of love become worshipers of God; we are given gifts by God to declare the praises of God.

Leading worship requires the right heart, and the right development, but it also requires the power of the Holy Spirit. It must have God's power and anointing to have any impact. Being skilled might impress someone but only God's anointing can transform someone.

Musicianship and excellence unfortunately aren't enough; human effort doesn't compensate for the bankruptcy of the soul. The presence of God must be in our worship services and flowing from our hearts and lives. How we express our love for God is being witnessed by the world.

The cross reveals how great God's love is for us, our worship tells the world how much we love Him. Don't let the pressure to perform rob you of the joy in ministry. Jesus calls us to ministry because He has given it to us and His yoke is easy and His burden light. One of the hardest things for me to learn was embracing my own humanity and flaws in view of God's grace for me.

"God is still writing straight lines with crooked sticks," as Larry Osbourne says. Remember that God loves you, not based on your performance but based on Jesus' performance. God placed you in Christ and Christ is in you. You are perfectly accepted, loved and favored by the Father. This is good news. Leading worship is a privilege; it should never be done out of compulsion or obligation, but rather out of devotion and love. As you pursue the call of God in your life, don't try to be anyone else to impress people. Be who God designed you to be because you are in Christ. You are a Royal-Priest, in all things and at all times cultivate the attitude of a servant; this is the heart of Jesus and the evidence of true holiness. Have fun; take calculated risks and be sure to rest. Spend quality time reflecting; never lose sight of the One who has called you.

Your commitment to worship in private will always impact your public ministry. We minister to an audience of One. We are entrusted to lead and bless the people in His name, by standing in His presence, walking in His power and living a life of grace and love. May your seasons be long, may you be covered by His grace and empowered by His hand. May you lead God's people with skill, with integrity of heart, with an attitude of fun but more importantly, with L-O-V-E, until we get called home to sing and worship in eternity.

Acknowledgments

Thank you to Mickey Stonier for inspiring me and helping me work this idea out. Also thank you to Nicole and Dave Franco for your advice at the inception of this journey. Thanks to Anita Palmer for the pointers in writing and publishing as I got started. Thanks to Reesa Cooper for her willing and detailed improvements to this work, your help and friendship played a huge role in the completion of this project.

Thanks to Valerie Ellery for helping me find better ways to share these ideas and helping me find the right patterns for each chapter. Thanks to Rei Lopez for his idea on adding questions after each chapter and his inspired original art work when I started to manifest this project.

Special thanks to the pastors and churches that I have had the honor to serve with. Without your trust in me I never would have discovered my calling. To the leaders and mentors who have invested in me personally, believed in me given me so much insight and wisdom, I cannot thank you enough you are a part of these pages.

There are so many worship leaders around the world who have deeply impacted my thinking through their songs, blogs, teachings, live recordings and books- thank you for helping me grow.

To the teams I have been a part of; your passion for excellence and teachable spirit have kept me humbled and thankful. To the wonderful worship leaders that I have led with, thank you for allowing me to be a part of your life. Thank you for caring so deeply about the work of God and the relationships, which are the most important part of ministry.

Thank you to my friends that have encouraged me, spoken words of life over me, prayed for me, held my arms up, given me loving feedback to help me grow, served in the battle with me and constantly helped me remain steadfast and continue walking in the calling God has placed on my life.

Thank you to my parents who gave me love, care and space to find my place and for being an example of Christ and modeled it with their life and marriage.

Very special thank you to my amazing family: Deepest thank you to my lovely, my wife **Clara** who has stood by my side while I failed and learned in so many ways and loved me with so much kindness. God has taken this mess of a man through His school of brokenness and I am forever thankful that I know who I am in Christ because you have always been by my side. To my kids, **Charlize** and **Lucas**; you both help me live a life of worship as a father and remind me that real ministry happens at home.